DISCOVERING SHAPES

POLYGONS

DAVID L. STIENECKER

ART BY RICHARD MACCABE

BENCHMARK BOOKS

MARSHALL CAVENDISH
NEW YORK

Benchmark Books
Marshall Cavendish Corporation
99 White Plains Road
Tarrytown, New York 10591-9001

©Marshall Cavendish Corporation, 1997

Series created by Blackbirch Graphics, Inc.

Printed and bound in the United States.

Library of Congress Cataloging-in-Publication Data

Stienecker, David.
    Polygons / by David L. Stienecker: art by Richard Maccabe.
        p.   cm. — (Discovering shapes)
    Includes index.
    Summary: Identifies various kinds of polygons and uses activities, puzzles, and games to explore these shapes.
    ISBN 0-7614-0461-9 (lib. bdg.)
    1. Polygons—Juvenile literature. [1. Polygons. 2. Shape. 3. Amusements.] I. Maccabe, Richard, ill. II. Title. III. Series.
QA482.S693   1997
793.7'4—dc20
                                                96-3170
                                                CIP
                                                AC

Contents

■ ■ ■ ■ ■ ■ ■

The Many Sides of Polygons

Polygons are shapes with three or more sides. Polygons with all sides the same length and all angles the same size are called regular polygons. Polygons with sides of different lengths and angles of different sizes are called irregular polygons.

An angle is a shape formed by two lines that meet.

regular polygon

irregular polygon

How many kinds of polygons with different numbers of sides can you find in this polygon picture? Keep track on a piece of paper.

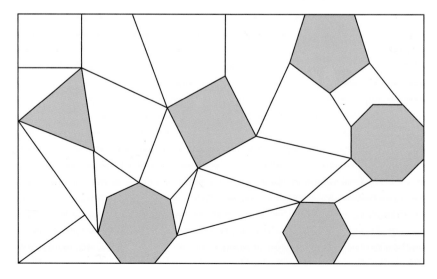

Polygons are named according to the number of sides they have. Here are the names of a few polygons. Try saying them aloud. Some of the names are pretty funny sounding.

Polygon	Number of sides	Name
	3	triangle
	4	quadrilateral
	5	pentagon
	6	hexagon
	7	heptagon
	8	octagon
	9	nonagon
	10	decagon
	11	ondecagon
	12	dodecagon

"Poly" means many and "gon" means angle. The word "polygon" means "many angles."

The world is full of polygons. See how many you can find.

A polygon has the same number of angles as it has sides.

• What are the names of the polygons you found in the picture? Were all the shapes polygons?

Block Letter Puzzles

Try this block letter puzzle. Make a copy of the polygons below. Then cut them out. Fit the pieces together to make this block letter:

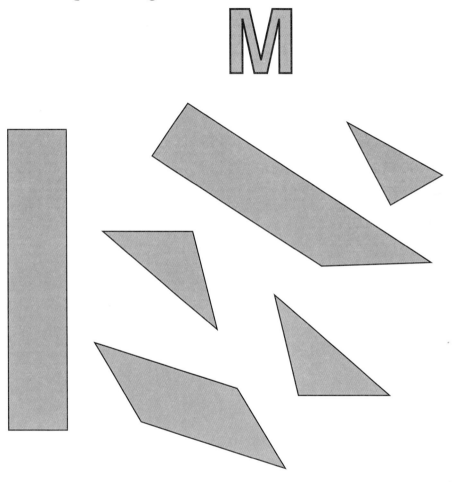

• Give the pieces to a friend. See how long it takes your friend to put them together.

• There are two kinds of polygons in the puzzle. Can you tell what they're called?

Here's another block letter puzzle to test your
new skills. Put these pieces together to make this
block letter:

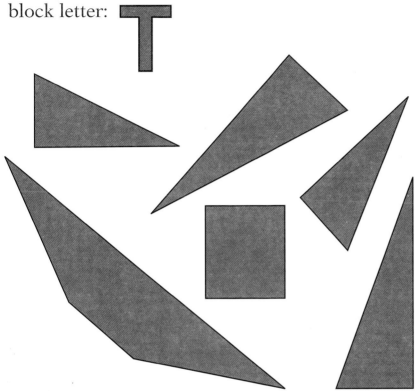

Try making some block letter puzzles of your own.

Here's what to do:

1. Draw the letter on a piece of graph paper.

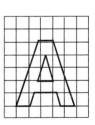

2. Draw lines to show how you want to cut
the letter into pieces. Be sure all the pieces
are polygons. No curved lines please.

3. Cut the pieces apart. That's all there is to it.

7

The World of Quadrilaterals

Quadrilaterals are polygons with four sides. Here are some special kinds of quadrilaterals. How many have you heard of?

Trapezoid

Only one pair of parallel sides.

Parallelogram

Two pairs of sides the same length. Both pairs of opposite sides parallel.

Rectangle

Two pairs of sides the same length. All angles right angles.

Square

All sides the same length. All angles right angles.

Rhombus

All sides the same length. Both pairs of opposite sides parallel.

Kite

Two pairs of touching sides the same length.

• Make copies of the quadrilaterals above. Then put them together to make different shapes.

• What other kinds of quadrilaterals can you draw? Remember, any shape with four sides is a quadrilateral.

Give this quadrilateral puzzle a try. Draw a large quadrilateral, any quadrilateral. Or, you can trace this one.

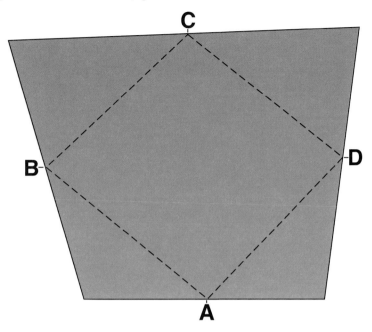

1. Use a ruler to find and mark the midpoint of each side of your quadrilateral. The midpoints on the quadrilateral above are labeled A, B, C, and D.

2. Connect each midpoint to make another quadrilateral inside the quadrilateral—like the dotted lines in the quadrilateral above.

3. Cut off the triangles formed at each corner. Don't throw away the remaining quadrilateral. You'll need it in the next step.

4. Now for the fun part. Try to place the four triangles so they exactly cover the remaining quadrilateral.

Try the puzzle with several different quadrilaterals. Try it with each of the special quadrilaterals on the opposite page.

Joining Hexagons

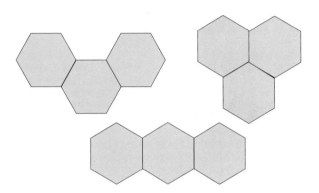

You can make some interesting shapes by joining hexagons, unless you only have two. This is the only way you can join two hexagons.

Things begin to get more interesting if you have three hexagons. There are three ways to join them.

With four hexagons, things really get interesting. There are seven ways to join them. Here are two. See if you can figure out the other five.

Flipping or rotating a shape doesn't count.

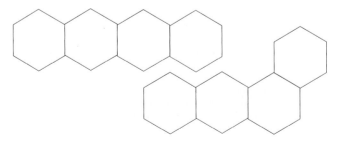

Make four regular hexagons out of construction paper or index cards. Then start putting them together in different ways. Good luck!

Think Polygons

Here's a polygon game you can play with two or more players. First, make two each of the following six cards.

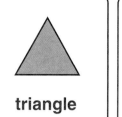 triangle

 quadrilateral

 pentagon

 hexagon

 heptagon

 octagon

How to play:

1. Mix up the cards. Then lay them face up in a 3 x 4 grid pattern like this. Give everyone 30 seconds to remember where the cards are. Then turn the cards over.

2. The first player turns two cards over. If the cards match, the player takes them and takes another turn. If they do not match, the cards are replaced face down and the next player takes a turn.

3. The game continues until all the cards are removed. The player with the most cards wins.

• You can make the game more difficult by adding pairs of cards. Just refer to the polygon chart on page 5.

11

Polygon Traceables

These figures are called traceables because you can start at one point and trace the entire figure without lifting your pencil or finger. You are not allowed to retrace any lines, but you can cross over them. Here are a couple of simple traceables to get you started.

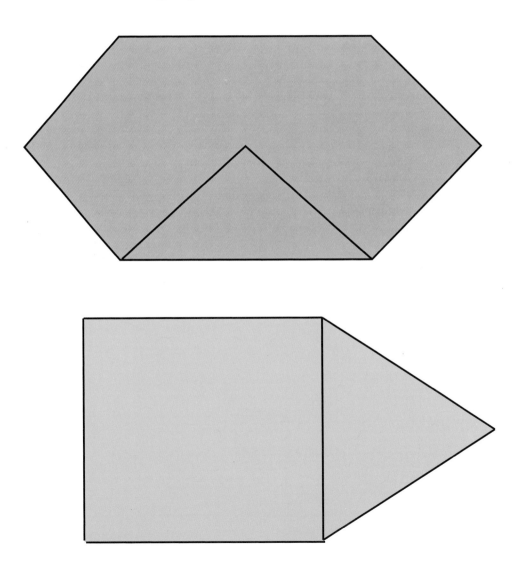

Now that you're all warmed up, try tracking these traceable traceables. Be patient. It might take several tries.

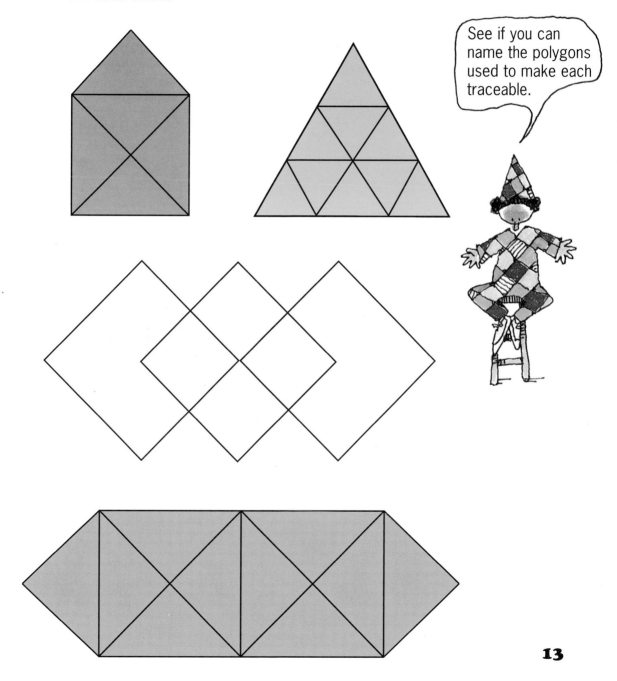

See if you can name the polygons used to make each traceable.

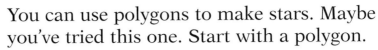

Making Stars

The star will have the same number of points as the polygon has sides.

You can use polygons to make stars. Maybe you've tried this one. Start with a polygon.

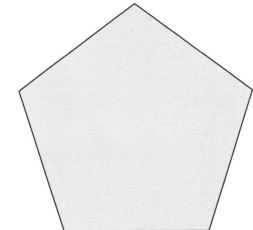

Then add some lines. Pretty soon you have a star.

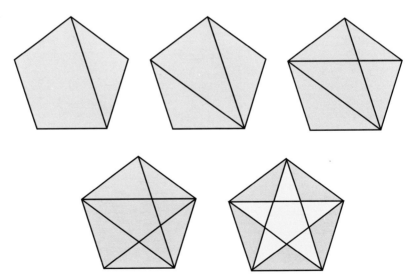

Note that the lines connect every other angle in the pentagon. That's because the pentagon has an odd number of sides.

Now try making a 6-pointed star, or hexagram, inside a hexagon. Half of the star has been made for you. Can you think of an easy way to finish the star?

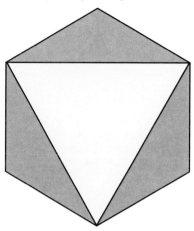

Now try making stars inside a heptagon and an octagon. You can trace these or make your own.

When the polygon has an even number of sides, you can make a star by drawing two overlapping figures.

• Once you've made your stars, try coloring them to make interesting designs. You can use them as decorations.

Did you notice that all the tans are polygons?

Tangram Polygons

Almost 4,000 years ago the Chinese made a puzzle by cutting a square into seven pieces. The puzzle is called a tangram. Each piece is called a tan. These are the seven tans in a tangram puzzle.

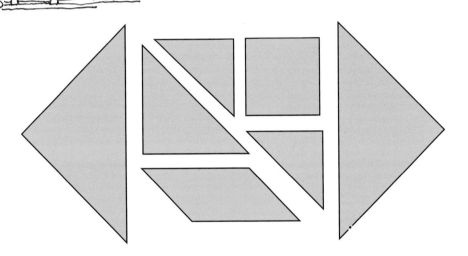

• Carefully trace or copy the tangram pieces above. Then cut them out. See if you can fit them together to make the square they originally came from. You must use all seven tans. Be patient, it may take a little time.

• Use all the tans to make a rectangle that is not a square.

• What are the names of the polygons that make up the tangram puzzle?

Now use the tans to make two other kinds of polygons. First see if you can fit all the tans into this parallelogram. They should fit inside with no leftover space.

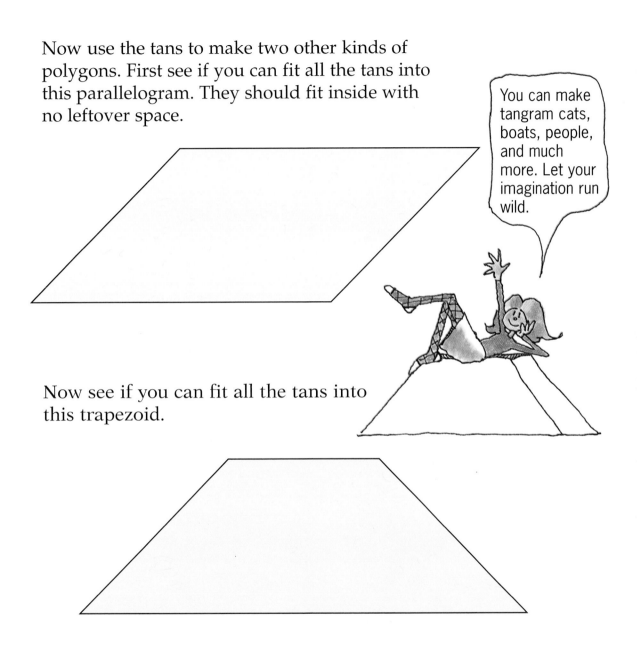

You can make tangram cats, boats, people, and much more. Let your imagination run wild.

Now see if you can fit all the tans into this trapezoid.

• People use tans to make all sorts of shapes and figures. In fact, more than 1,600 tangram designs have been invented. There are even books about it. So have fun and experiment for awhile. See what shapes and figures you can make.

17

Polygon Fold-ups

Did you know that snowflakes are shaped like hexagons? If you looked at a snowflake under a magnifying glass it might look something like this. Can you make out the six sides?

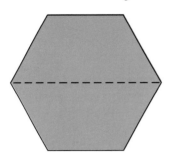

Make a polygon fold-up snowflake. Begin with a large hexagon.

Fold it along the dotted line so it looks like this.

Fold again along the dotted line so it looks like this.

Then make cuts all around the edges. The more cuts you make, the more interesting your snowflake will be.

Unfold your hexagon and you have a snowflake. Can you still make out the hexagon shape?

Use other kinds of polygons to make fold-ups. Of course, you won't end up with a snowflake. But you'll have a lot of fun. Try this polygon fold-up.

Begin with a triangle.

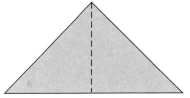

Fold it along the dotted line so it looks like this. Keep folding to make smaller and smaller triangles.

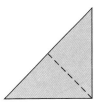

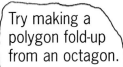
Try making a polygon fold-up from an octagon.

Then make cuts all around the edges as you did for the snowflake.

Unfold your triangle and see what you've made.

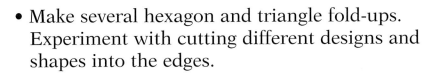

- Make several hexagon and triangle fold-ups. Experiment with cutting different designs and shapes into the edges.

- Use your polygon fold-ups to make things. Paste them onto sheets of colored paper to make place mats. Hang them from thread to decorate your room. Use them to decorate gift packages and greeting cards.

Fun with Pentagrams

A pentagram is a 5-pointed star. It is also a decagon because it has ten sides. In the past, pentagrams were a symbol of magical power. They were sometimes used to keep evil away and to attract good. Here's an unusual way to make a pentagram.

1. Begin with a strip of paper about an inch wide and $11\frac{1}{2}$ inches long.

2. Tie the paper strip into a knot and press it flat so it looks like this.

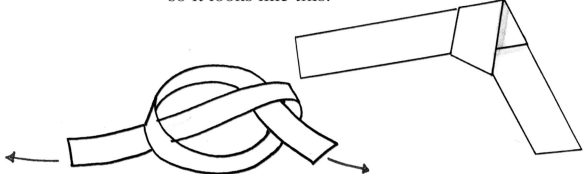

3. Fold over one end of the strip and hold it up to a strong light. Look for the pentagram.

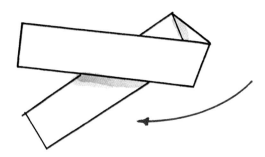

Here's a neat puzzle using a pentagram. You will need four small markers, such as four pennies, beans, or buttons. Oh yes, you'll also need a pentagon. You can use this one.

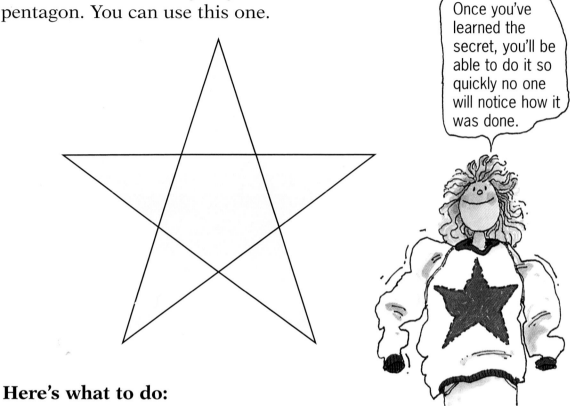

Once you've learned the secret, you'll be able to do it so quickly no one will notice how it was done.

Here's what to do:

1. Put a marker on any point of the star. Then slide it along one of the black lines to another star point and leave it there.

2. Put a second marker on any empty star point. Slide it along a black line to another empty point and leave it there.

3. Do the same with the third and fourth markers. The idea is to have all four markers on different points of the star. It's not as easy as it sounds.

21

Polygon Designs

Polygons can be used to make interesting designs. Here is one polygon design made with a parallelogram and one made with a rhombus.

Here are two other designs that are each made with a single kind of polygon. What polygon was used to make each one?

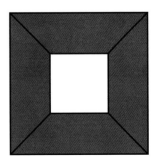

These designs are made with more than one kind of polygon. What kind of polygons were used to make each design?

Make your polygons with colored paper, or use markers to color them.

Make copies of these polygons. Put them together to make the designs on these pages. Then try making some designs of your own.

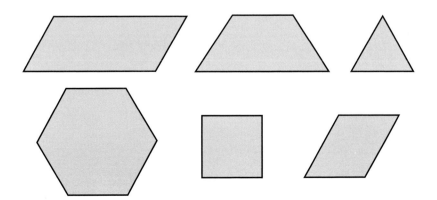

Polygon Changes

These shapes are all polygons. But with one simple cut you can change them into other polygons.

Here's what to do:

1. Copy or carefully trace the shape onto a piece of paper. Then cut it out.

2. Cut the shape into two pieces. If you cut it just right, you should be able to put the two pieces together to make the polygon shown on each shape. Good luck!

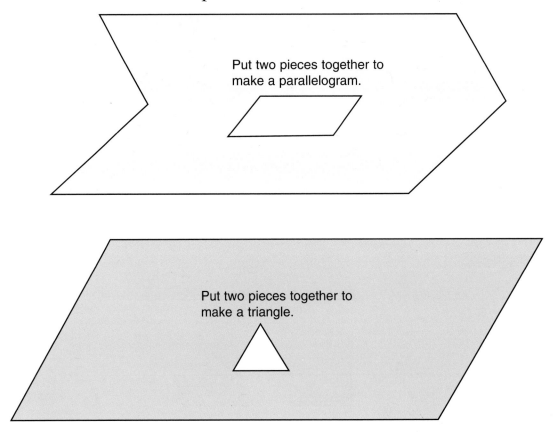

Put two pieces together to make a parallelogram.

Put two pieces together to make a triangle.

Put two pieces together to make a pentagon.

You can flip, turn, or rotate the pieces to make them fit.

Put two pieces together to make a trapezoid.

Put two pieces together to make a hexagon.

25

PolyMaze

There are all kinds of mazes. But have you ever seen one made with polygons? See how long it takes you to get through this polymaze.

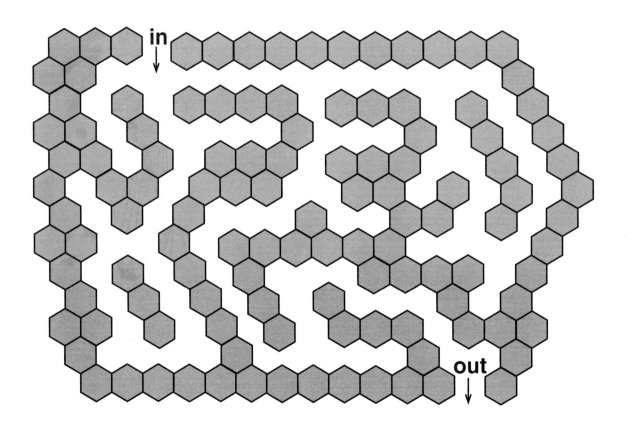

• What kind of polygon was used to make the polymaze?

• Try making a polymaze of your own. Decide what kind of polygon you want to use. Then lay out your maze. Give it to a friend to solve.

Answers

Pp. 4–5, The Many Sides of Polygons

All of the shapes in the polygon picture are polygons. The picture contains one or more of the following: triangle, quadrilateral, pentagon, hexagon, heptagon, and octagon.

Pp. 6–7, Block Letter Puzzles

Both puzzles are made up of quadrilaterals and triangles.

Pp. 8–9, The World of Quadrilaterals
No answers.

P. 10, Joining Hexagons

P. 11. Think Polygons
No answers.

Pp. 12–13, Polygon Traceables

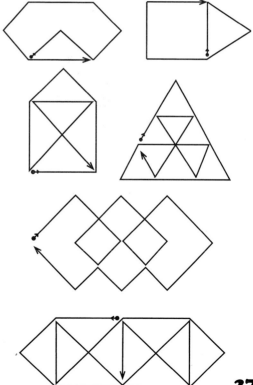

Pp. 14–15, Making Stars

You can finish the hexagram by making another triangle and flipping it:

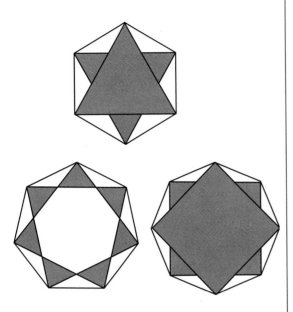

Pp. 16–17, Tangram Polygrams

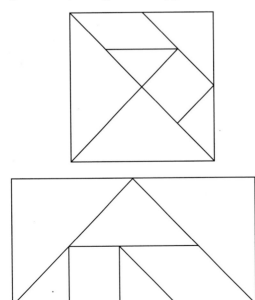

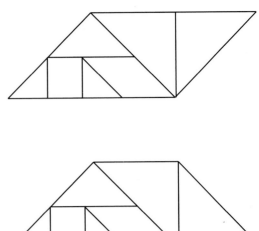

Pp. 18–19, Polygon Fold-ups

No answers.

Pp. 20–21, Fun with Pentagrams

If you "tied" your paper knot in just the right way, you should be able to see this pentagram when you hold the paper knot up to a strong light.

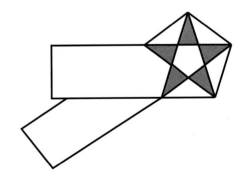

28

When you tried the pentagram puzzle you may have found that there was no place to put the last marker. Here's the secret.

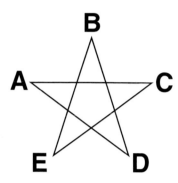

Place the marker so it can be slid to the star point where the previous marker was. Here's an example:

1. Place a marker on A and slide it to C.

2. The previous marker was on A, so place a marker on D and slide it to A.

3. The previous marker was on D, so place a marker on B and slide it to D.

4. The previous marker was on B, so place a marker on E and slide it to B.

Pps. 22–23, Polygon Designs

This design was made with 14 triangles.

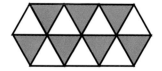

This design was made with 4 trapezoids.

This design was made with 4 squares and 8 triangles.

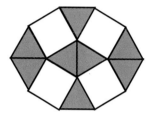

This design was made with 6 squares, 6 triangles, and 1 hexagon.

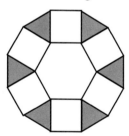

This design was made with 6 triangles and 1 hexagon.

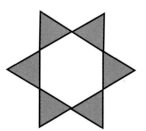

Pps. 24–25, Polygon Changes

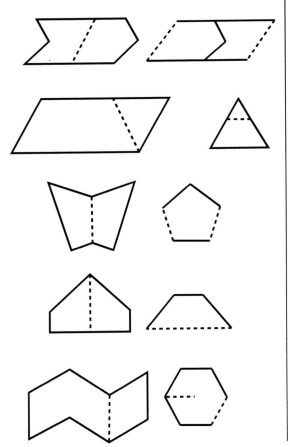

p. 26, Polymaze

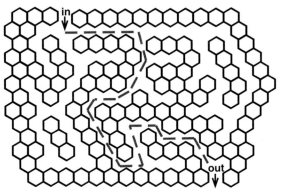

Glossary

angle A shape formed by two lines that meet.

heptagon A polygon with seven sides.

hexagon A polygon with six sides.

hexagram A six-pointed star.

irregular polygon A polygon with sides of different lengths and angles of different sizes.

midpoint A point that divides a line in half.

octagon A polygon with eight sides.

parallelogram A quadrilateral with two pairs of parallel sides.

pentagon A polygon with five sides.

pentagram A five-pointed star.

polygon A figure with three or more lines joined at the endpoints.

quadrilateral A polygon with four sides.

rectangle A parallelogram with four right angles.

regular polygon A polygon with all sides the same length and all angles the same size.

rhombus A parallelogram with all sides the same length.

rotate To turn a figure about its center.

square A rectangle with all four sides the same length.

tangram A puzzle made by cutting a square into seven pieces.

trapezoid A quadrilateral with only one pair of parallel sides.

triangle A polygon with three sides.

Index